Setting No Wicked Thing Before My Eyes

Biblical Discernment in a Compromised World

Eld Joel Latimore Jr.

Setting No Wicked Thing Before My Eyes

Biblical Discernment in a Compromised World

Written by Eld Joel Latimore Jr.

EPIGRAPH

"I will set no wicked thing before mine eyes...

A froward heart shall depart from me:

I will not know a wicked person."

Psalm 101:3–4

TABLE OF CONTENTS

DEDICATION

This book is dedicated to the young men and women who were never taught how to guard their hearts, who learned life through exposure instead of instruction, and who were shaped by voices louder than wisdom.

To those who grew up without guidance, without protection at the gates of the mind, and without anyone explaining how influence works— this is for you.

This book is not written to condemn you for where you are, but to show you how a different path begins.

Not by pretending the past did not happen, but by learning what should have been taught from the beginning.

It is also dedicated to parents, mentors, and leaders who now recognize what was missed, and who are willing to tell the truth, take responsibility, and choose to teach the next generation more carefully.

May these pages help close gates that were left open, strengthen hearts that were left unguarded, and point every reader toward wisdom, discernment, and the possibility of a changed walk.

PREFACE

There is a verse in Scripture that is short, quiet, and often overlooked—but it explains far more about our lives than we may realize.

"I will set no wicked thing before mine eyes…

A froward heart shall depart from me:

I will not know a wicked person."

(Psalm 101:3–4)

These words were written long before social media, music streaming, television, or video games. Yet they speak directly to the world we live in now, because they address something timeless: **how influence enters a life and shapes a heart.**

The Bible never presents evil as something that appears suddenly or without warning. Scripture teaches that destruction begins quietly—through what we see, what we hear, what we allow, and who we walk with. Long before a choice becomes an action, it becomes a thought. Long before a thought becomes a habit, it becomes agreement.

Many of us were never taught this.

We were taught how to survive.

We were taught how to react.

We were taught how to fit in, how to be tough, how to protect ourselves.

But we were not taught how to **guard the gates of the heart.**

God commanded parents to teach their children diligently—to explain right and wrong, to warn them before harm, to guide them when temptation came, and to show them how to walk wisely. When that instruction was missing, other teachers stepped in. The streets taught. The screens taught. The music taught. The crowd taught.

This book was written to explain what should have been taught.

It is not written to shame those who are incarcerated, struggling, or trying to rebuild their lives. It is written to tell the truth plainly: **what we allow before our eyes, into our ears, and out of our mouths shapes the direction of our lives.** Influence is never neutral. Agreement always leads somewhere.

Psalm 101 is not about perfection. It is about **intentional living.** It is about recognizing that the heart does not protect itself—and that if we do not decide what is allowed in, something else will decide for us.

This book will walk through Scripture to show how influence works, how the Bible identifies the gates of the heart, and how a different path begins—not with excuses, but with understanding and responsibility. Freedom does not start when a cell door opens. It starts when the mind learns to discern.

If this book helps you recognize what shaped your thinking, understand how your path was formed, and see that God still offers wisdom for a new walk—then it has done what it was written to do.

INTRODUCTION

Most people don't wake up one day and decide to ruin their lives.

They don't plan to lose their freedom, break their families' hearts, or end up behind locked doors. What usually happens is quieter than that. A path is formed over time—through what is seen, what is heard, what is repeated, and who is walked with.

The Bible explains this in ways many of us were never taught.

God never expected children to raise themselves or to figure life out by trial and error. He commanded parents to teach, to warn, to correct, and to guide. When that instruction is missing— or inconsistent—something else steps in to do the teaching. And whatever teaches you long enough eventually shapes how you think, how you react, and how you choose.

This book is not about blaming parents, culture, or circumstances. It is about **understanding influence.** Because you cannot change a path you don't understand.

Psalm 101:3–4 shows us that life is shaped at the **entry points of the heart**—what we allow before our eyes, what we tolerate around us, and who we agree to walk with. Scripture teaches that these things do not stay on the outside. They move inward. They form thoughts. Thoughts become attitudes. Attitudes become actions.

By the time consequences show up, the real work has already been done—inside.

Many young people grow up learning how to react, how to survive, and how to protect themselves, but never learn how to **guard their inner life.** Nobody explains that the eyes, ears, and mouth are gates. Nobody explains that repetition trains the mind. Nobody explains that agreement happens before action.

This book is written to explain those things plainly, using Scripture—not opinions.

It is not written to excuse wrong choices. Responsibility matters. But responsibility makes more sense when truth is understood. God does not only judge actions—He teaches wisdom. And wisdom begins with discernment.

As you read, you may recognize patterns in your own life. You may see how certain influences shaped your thinking long before you ever made a decision that brought consequences. That awareness is not meant to crush you—it is meant to **free you.**

You cannot undo the past. But you can learn how to walk differently going forward.

This book is about learning how to guard what enters the heart, how to recognize influence before it becomes agreement, and how Scripture offers a wiser path—even now.

CHAPTER 1

SETTING THE FIRST BOUNDARY

"I will set no wicked thing before mine eyes."

— Psalm 101:3

Every path begins with a first boundary.

Before there is a crime, before there is a bad decision, before there is a consequence, there is **exposure.** Something is seen. Something is heard. Something is allowed. Scripture does not describe destruction as sudden—it describes it as **entered.**

David does not say, *"I will never do wicked things."*

He says, *"I will not set them before my eyes."*

That distinction matters.

The Bible teaches that the heart does not create evil out of nothing. It is **fed.** And whatever feeds the heart long enough will eventually shape how a person thinks, reacts, and chooses.

"Keep thy heart with all diligence; for out of it are the issues of life."

— Proverbs 4:23 (KJV)

Most of us were never taught this.

We were taught how to avoid trouble—
sometimes.

We were taught how to survive.

We were taught how to respond when
disrespected.

But we were not taught how **influence works.**

The Eye Is Not Neutral

Jesus said:

"The light of the body is the eye: therefore when thine eye is single, thy whole body also is full of light; but when thine eye is evil, thy body also is full of darkness."

— Luke 11:34 (KJV)

That means the eye is not just a camera.

It is a **gate.**

What enters through the eyes does not stay on the surface. It travels inward—to the imagination, to desire, to thought patterns, and eventually to action.

This is why David begins with the eyes. If the eye gate is unguarded, the heart will be shaped without permission.

Scripture confirms this connection:

"Mine eye affecteth mine heart."

— **Lamentations 3:51 (KJV)**

This is not about being perfect.

It is about being **intentional.**

What Does "Setting" Mean?

David says, *"I will set no wicked thing before mine eyes."* **(Psalm 101:3).**

To set something means:

- to place it there

- to keep it there

- to return to it

- to give it space

This includes:

- what you watch repeatedly

- what you scroll through

- what you choose to focus on

- what you allow to entertain you

Many influences don't force their way in. They are **invited.**

The Bible warns about this kind of exposure:

"Make no provision for the flesh, to fulfil the lusts thereof."

— Romans 13:14 (KJV)

And many people never realize that they are training their own minds.

The Heart Follows What the Eyes Lead

Scripture teaches that behavior is not random—it flows from within.

"For out of the heart proceed evil thoughts, murders, adulteries, fornications…"

— Matthew 15:19 (KJV)

But the heart cannot be guarded if the gates are ignored.

When violent images, sexual content, disrespect, revenge, greed, or lawlessness are seen over and over, they stop feeling shocking. They begin to feel **normal.** And when something feels normal, the heart no longer resists it.

Scripture describes this progression clearly:

"Then when lust hath conceived, it bringeth forth sin: and sin, when it is finished, bringeth forth death."

— James 1:15 (KJV)

This is how influence works:

- Exposure removes shock

- Repetition removes resistance

- Agreement removes restraint

By the time action happens, the heart has already been trained.

Why This Matters for Your Life

Many people behind bars were never taught to guard the eye gate. They grew up watching things that trained anger, lust, impulsiveness, and retaliation—long before they ever acted on those thoughts.

That does not remove responsibility.

But it **explains the process.**

God is not surprised by this. That is why
Scripture repeatedly calls people to watchfulness:

*"Watch and pray, that ye enter not into
temptation."*

— Matthew 26:41 (KJV)

David understood something many never learn:

If I don't choose what comes in, something else
will choose for me.

A Boundary Is Not a Cage

Setting a boundary is not weakness.

It is **wisdom.**

"He that hath no rule over his own spirit is like a city that is broken down, and without walls."

— Proverbs 25:28 (KJV)

This book is not asking you to pretend you live in a perfect world. It is teaching you how to live **carefully** in a broken one.

"See then that ye walk circumspectly, not as fools, but as wise."

— Ephesians 5:15 (KJV)

Psalm 101 does not begin with judgment.

It begins with a decision.

And every different path begins the same way.

Closing Charge

What you allow before your eyes is not harmless.

It is training.

You may not have chosen what you were first exposed to, but you are now responsible for what you continue to allow.

"All things are lawful for me, but all things are not expedient."

— 1 Corinthians 6:12 (KJV)

If you want a different path, it starts with a boundary.

And every boundary starts with a decision.

Reflective Summary

Psalm 101:3 teaches that destruction does not begin with action, but with exposure. The eyes are a gate to the heart, and what is repeatedly seen shapes imagination, desire, and behavior.

Scripture confirms that the heart follows what the eyes lead **(Proverbs 4:23; Matthew 15:19).**

When the eye gate is left unguarded, the heart is formed without intention. Setting boundaries is not about perfection—it is about wisdom, responsibility, and choosing direction before consequences appear.

Reflective Questions

1. What are some things I have repeatedly set before my eyes without considering their effect on my heart? **(Psalm 101:3)**

2. Can I see a connection between what I watched or focused on and how I learned to think or react? **(Lamentations 3:51)**

3. What did no one ever explain to me about guarding my eyes while I was growing up? **(Proverbs 4:23)**

4. What is one boundary I know I need to set to protect my heart moving forward? **(Proverbs 25:28)**

5. Do I believe it is possible to choose a different path starting with what I allow into my life now? **(Ephesians 5:15)**

Prayer

Lord,

I acknowledge that my heart has been shaped by many things I did not understand at the time.

I ask You now for wisdom to see clearly and courage to make better choices.

Teach me how to guard my eyes and to recognize what is harmful before it takes root in my heart.

Help me to walk with intention, discipline, and understanding. Give me strength to choose what leads to life.

In Jesus Name, Amen.

CHAPTER 2

GUARDING THE EAR GATE

"Take heed therefore how ye hear."

— **Luke 8:18 (KJV)**

If the eyes are a gate to the heart, **then the ears are also a gate.**

What enters through the ears does not remain outside. Words, voices, and repeated messages pass inward, shaping belief, forming agreement, and influencing direction.

Scripture places heavy responsibility on hearing because **hearing shapes belief, belief shapes agreement, and agreement shapes action.**

Before a person acts, they are convinced.

Before they are convinced, they have been listening.

That is why Jesus did not say, *"Take heed what you hear,"* but,

"Take heed how ye hear."

— Luke 8:18 (KJV)

The issue is not only exposure—it is reception. What the ear gate allows in is either examined or absorbed.

Hearing Is a Form of Training

Scripture is clear:

"So then faith cometh by hearing, and hearing by the word of God."

— Romans 10:17 (KJV)

If faith can be built by hearing, then so can fear, anger, lust, pride, rebellion, and violence. Hearing is not neutral. Whatever is repeatedly allowed through the ear gate **trains the inner life.**

This is why Scripture repeatedly warns about voices:

"Be not deceived: evil communications corrupt good manners."

— 1 Corinthians 15:33 (KJV)

Corruption does not begin with behavior. It begins with **conversation**—what is heard, repeated, and accepted.

What the Ear Gate Allows In

The ear gate includes:

- music and lyrics

- conversations and jokes

- advice and counsel

- repeated messages

- voices you trust or admire

Many young people were never taught to question what they were hearing. They were taught to accept it, repeat it, and live by it.

Scripture warns about this danger:

"The ear that heareth the reproof of life abideth among the wise."

— Proverbs 15:31 (KJV)

If wisdom comes from hearing correction, then destruction comes from rejecting it.

Voices Shape Agreement

The Bible teaches that agreement always comes before direction.

"Can two walk together, except they be agreed?"

— Amos 3:3 (KJV)

Agreement is often formed through hearing. When a voice is heard long enough, it begins to sound reasonable. When it sounds reasonable, it begins to feel right. When it feels right, it is acted upon.

This is how influence becomes agreement—and agreement becomes action.

Scripture warns about this progression:

"For the time will come when they will not endure sound doctrine; but after their own lusts shall they heap to themselves teachers, having itching ears."

— 2 Timothy 4:3 (KJV)

People do not always listen to what is true. They often listen to what **confirms what they already want.**

The Ear and the Heart Are Connected

What enters the ears settles in the heart.

"Incline thine ear unto wisdom, and apply thine heart to understanding."

— Proverbs 2:2 (KJV)

This is why Scripture pairs hearing with responsibility:

"He that hath ears to hear, let him hear."

— Matthew 11:15 (KJV)

Hearing is not passive. It is a **choice.**

When anger, disrespect, revenge, sexual immorality, or lawlessness are constantly spoken, celebrated, or joked about, they stop sounding wrong. The heart becomes familiar with them—and familiarity removes resistance.

Why This Matters for Your Life

Many incarcerated youth were trained by voices long before they were trained by wisdom. The streets spoke. Music spoke. Friends spoke. Survival spoke. But correction, restraint, and discernment were often silent.

That does not excuse wrongdoing.

But it **explains how the mind was shaped.**

God addresses this directly:

"Hear instruction, and be wise, and refuse it not."

— **Proverbs 8:33 (KJV)**

If a person does not choose which voices to hear, the loudest voices will choose for them.

Choosing a Different Voice

Guarding the ear gate does not mean silence.

It means **selection.**

Scripture gives direction:

"Let the word of Christ dwell in you richly."

— Colossians 3:16 (KJV)

What dwells in you will eventually guide you, shape you, and speak through you.

A changed path begins when a person decides to **listen differently.**

Closing Charge

What you hear repeatedly is shaping you—whether you realize it or not.

You may not have chosen the voices that first influenced you, but you can choose what you continue to listen to now.

"Incline your ear, and come unto me: hear, and your soul shall live."

— Isaiah 55:3 (KJV)

If you want a different direction, you must allow a different voice.

Reflective Summary

Scripture teaches that hearing is a powerful gate to the heart. Faith, belief, and agreement are all shaped by what a person hears repeatedly **(Romans 10:17; Amos 3:3).**

The ear gate trains the mind long before actions occur. When voices that promote sin, anger, or rebellion are accepted without discernment, the heart becomes aligned with them.

Guarding the ear gate is an essential step in choosing wisdom, direction, and life.

Reflective Questions

1. What voices have influenced my thinking the most over time? **(1 Corinthians 15:33)**

2. Have I noticed certain words, messages, or lyrics shaping how I react or speak? **(Matthew 12:34)**

3. What kind of voices did I listen to when I was forming my values? **(Proverbs 2:2)**

4. What voices do I need to limit or remove to guard my heart more carefully? **(2 Timothy 4:3)**

5. What godly instruction or truth do I need to start listening to more intentionally? **(Colossians 3:16)**

Prayer

Lord,

Your Word tells me to take heed how I hear. I confess that many voices have shaped my thinking without wisdom or truth.

Teach me to recognize which voices lead me away from You and which ones bring life.

Help me to guard my ear gate, to receive correction, and to choose instruction that leads to understanding.

Fill my heart with Your truth and guide my steps in the right direction.

In Jesus' Name, Amen.

CHAPTER 3

GUARDING THE MOUTH GATE

"Out of the abundance of the heart the mouth speaketh."

— Matthew 12:34 (KJV)

The mouth is also a **gate.**

What enters the heart through the eyes and the ears does not remain hidden. It eventually looks for expression, and the mouth is where agreement is released.

Scripture teaches that words are not harmless sounds or emotional releases; they are **commitments** that shape direction.

Before a life changes course, language changes course.

Before behavior becomes fixed, speech becomes familiar.

That is why the Bible speaks so often—and so seriously—about the tongue.

The Mouth Reveals What Has Filled the Heart

Jesus said plainly:

"For out of the abundance of the heart the mouth speaketh."

— Matthew 12:34 (KJV)

The mouth does not invent what it says. It reveals what the heart has already absorbed. What entered through the eye gate and ear gate eventually shows up in speech.

Scripture confirms this connection:

"A good man out of the good treasure of his heart bringeth forth that which is good; and an evil man... that which is evil."

— Luke 6:45 (KJV)

Speech exposes agreement long before action appears.

Confession Is Not Optional — It Is Binding

Scripture teaches that confession is not optional—it is binding. **Romans 10:9–11** shows that belief alone is not the end; confession with the mouth completes agreement.

"That if thou shalt confess with thy mouth the Lord Jesus, and shalt believe in thine heart that God hath raised him from the dead, thou shalt be saved.

For with the heart man believeth unto righteousness; and with the mouth confession is made unto salvation."

— Romans 10:9–10 (KJV)

With the heart a person believes, but with the mouth commitment is made. This means words are not just expressions—they are **contracts.**

What a person repeatedly confesses aligns the heart with a direction and pulls life toward that outcome.

Scripture warns of this reality:

"Thou art snared with the words of thy mouth."
— **Proverbs 6:2 (KJV)**

The mouth does not merely speak—it **binds.**

The Power of the Tongue

The Bible is unmistakable:

"Death and life are in the power of the tongue."

— **Proverbs 18:21 (KJV)**

Words can justify anger, normalize violence, excuse sin, or reinforce hopelessness. Many young people learned to speak survival language—threats, disrespect, bravado, retaliation—long before they learned restraint or wisdom.

James writes:

"Behold, how great a matter a little fire kindleth!

And the tongue is a fire…"

— James 3:5–6 (KJV)

The tongue sets direction. It escalates conflict or restrains it. It hardens the heart or begins to heal it.

Speech Trains the Heart

What is spoken repeatedly becomes familiar, and what is familiar becomes acceptable.

Scripture commands:

"Let no corrupt communication proceed out of your mouth, but that which is good to the use of edifying."

— Ephesians 4:29 (KJV)

When violent, immoral, or disrespectful speech is repeated, the heart becomes comfortable with those ideas. Familiarity removes resistance. Over time, speech becomes permission.

The Bible states the outcome clearly:

"A man's belly shall be satisfied with the fruit of his mouth."

— Proverbs 18:20 (KJV)

You eventually live with what you say.

Why This Matters for Your Life

Many incarcerated youths confessed anger before acting on it.

They confessed retaliation before violence.

They confessed identity—*"this is just who I am"*—before living it.

They did not realize they were **agreeing with a future.**

That does not excuse wrongdoing.

But it explains how reactions were trained.

God gives this instruction:

"Set a watch, O LORD, before my mouth; keep the door of my lips."

— Psalm 141:3 (KJV)

A guarded mouth helps retrain a guarded heart.

Changing the Agreement

Guarding the mouth gate does not mean silence.

It means **discipline** and **intention.**

"Let your speech be alway with grace, seasoned with salt."

— **Colossians 4:6 (KJV)**

The same mouth that binds can also release. A different confession supports a different direction.

Closing Charge

What you speak reinforces what you believe.

You may not have chosen the words you learned early in life, but you are responsible for the words you speak now.

"Whoso keepeth his mouth and his tongue keepeth his soul from troubles."

— **Proverbs 21:23 (KJV)**

If you want a different outcome, you must guard what you release.

Reflective Summary

Scripture teaches that the mouth is a powerful gate connected directly to the heart **(Matthew 12:34)**.

Confession is not optional but binding; with the heart a person believes, and with the mouth agreement is sealed **(Romans 10:9–10)**.

Words act as contracts that shape direction and influence outcomes **(Proverbs 18:21)**. Guarding the mouth gate is essential for retraining the heart and choosing a wiser path forward.

Reflective Questions

1. What words do I speak most often when I am angry, stressed, or challenged? **(Matthew 12:34)**

2. Can I see a connection between what I repeatedly confess and the direction my life has taken? **(Proverbs 18:21)**

3. What identity statements have I spoken that may have shaped my choices? **(Proverbs 6:2)**

4. How does **Romans 10:9–11** change the way I think about the power of confession?

5. What new words or confessions would support the direction I want my life to take? **(Colossians 4:6)**

Prayer

Lord,

Your Word teaches that my words matter and that confession seals agreement.

I ask You to help me guard the door of my lips and to speak with wisdom, truth, and restraint.

Break agreements I have made with **anger, fear, and hopelessness,** and help me to confess **life, discipline**, and **truth.**

Align my speech with Your Word and guide my steps into a better path.

In Jesus' Name, Amen.

CHAPTER 4

WHO IS SHAPING THE GATES?

"Be not deceived: evil communications corrupt good manners."

— 1 Corinthians 15:33 (KJV)

No gate shapes itself.

If the eyes, ears, and mouth are gates to the heart, then an important question must be asked:

Who is standing at those gates—and why?

The Bible warns repeatedly that influence is not random and that deception often comes dressed as entertainment, freedom, or choice. Scripture does not assume that people are always led astray by ignorance alone; it teaches that many are **intentionally influenced.**

"For they have sown the wind, and they shall reap the whirlwind."

— Hosea 8:7 (KJV)

What is sown into the heart will eventually be reaped in life.

Industries That Profit From Access

There are powerful industries that invest enormous time, money, and creativity into capturing the attention of youth. These industries are not neutral, and they are not concerned with spiritual development, moral character, or long-term consequences.

Their goal is simple: **access.**

Access to the eye gate.

Access to the ear gate.

Access to identity, emotion, and reaction.

Scripture warns:

"Woe unto them that call evil good, and good evil; that put darkness for light, and light for darkness."

— Isaiah 5:20 (KJV)

When destructive behavior is normalized and packaged as entertainment, the heart is trained without permission.

The Eye Gate and Visual Conditioning

Images are powerful teachers.

Violence, sexual immorality, disrespect for authority, greed, and revenge are often presented visually in ways that remove shock and consequences.

Repeated exposure through screens trains the eye to accept what Scripture warns against.

"Mine eye affecteth mine heart."

— Lamentations 3:51 (KJV)

When the eye sees lawlessness rewarded and righteousness mocked, the heart quietly adjusts its expectations.

The Ear Gate and Repeated Messaging

Words shape belief.

Music, dialogue, jokes, and repeated phrases enter through the ear gate and begin forming agreement.

When messages of **anger, retaliation, lust,** and **hopelessness** are repeated often enough, they stop sounding wrong and start sounding normal.

"Take heed therefore how ye hear."

— Luke 8:18 (KJV)

Scripture does not say to stop hearing—but to **be careful how hearing is received.**

The Mouth Gate and Identity Reinforcement

What is seen and heard eventually comes out of the mouth.

Youth are encouraged—often without realizing it—to **repeat phrases, slogans, attitudes,** and **identities** that reinforce **rebellion, anger,** or **hopelessness**. Over time, confession becomes agreement, and agreement becomes direction.

"Death and life are in the power of the tongue."

— Proverbs 18:21 (KJV)

Industries may not force anyone to speak—but they provide the language that many adopt.

Why These Influences Do Not Care

These systems do not know the names of the youth they influence. They do not attend court dates. They do not visit jail cells. They do not sit with families after consequences arrive.

Scripture explains this clearly:

"The thief cometh not, but for to steal, and to kill, and to destroy."

— John 10:10 (KJV)

Once access is gained and profit is made, the damage is left behind.

Not Ignorance—Discernment Was Missing

Many youths were not stupid or reckless. They were **uninstructed.**

They were never taught:

- how influence works

- how repetition trains the mind

- how agreement forms quietly

- how gates must be guarded

Scripture speaks to this condition:

"My people are destroyed for lack of knowledge."

— Hosea 4:6 (KJV)

This book exists to supply that missing instruction.

God's Call to Discernment

God does not call His people to isolation—but to discernment.

"Prove all things; hold fast that which is good."

— 1 Thessalonians 5:21 (KJV)

When youth learn how the gates work, they can begin to choose differently—not perfectly, but wisely.

Closing Charge

Not everything offered to you was meant for your good.

You were influenced by systems that wanted access, not your wellbeing. But understanding how those systems work gives you power to choose differently.

"Be wise as serpents, and harmless as doves."

— Matthew 10:16 (KJV)

Wisdom begins with discernment.

Reflective Summary

Scripture teaches that influence is intentional and powerful. Industries that profit from attention gain access through the gates of the eyes, ears, and mouth, shaping thought patterns and normalizing behavior without regard for consequences **(Isaiah 5:20; 1 Corinthians 15:33).**

Many youths were never taught how these influences work. God calls His people to discernment—not isolation—so that they can guard their hearts and choose a wiser path.

Reflective Questions

1. What messages have I repeatedly seen or heard that shaped how I think about violence, respect, or identity? **(Lamentations 3:51)**

2. Did anyone ever explain to me how these influences affect the heart and mind? **(Hosea 4:6)**

3. Can I see how repetition made certain behaviors feel normal over time? **(Luke 8:18)**

4. Who benefits from the messages I was consuming—and who pays the price? **(John 10:10)**

5. What gates do I need to guard more
carefully going forward? **(Proverbs 4:23)**

Prayer

Lord,

I ask You to give me discernment. Help me see clearly how I was influenced and why certain paths felt normal to me.

Open my understanding so I can guard my heart and make wiser choices.

Teach me to recognize what does not come from You and to choose what leads to life.

Guide my steps forward with wisdom and clarity.

In the name of Jesus, Amen.

CHAPTER 5

REPETITION, DESENSITIZATION, AND THE SLOW DRIFT

"Know ye not, that to whom ye yield yourselves servants to obey, his servants ye are to whom ye obey?"

— Romans 6:16 (KJV)

Most damage does not happen all at once.

It happens **slowly.**

Scripture teaches that destruction is rarely
sudden. It is usually the result of **yielding,
repetition,** and **gradual agreement.**

What is seen, heard, and spoken repeatedly does
not remain neutral—it becomes familiar. And
what becomes familiar begins to feel acceptable.

This is the danger of repetition.

Repetition Trains the Heart

The Bible explains that the heart is shaped by what it is **continually exposed to.**

"While they promise them liberty, they themselves are the servants of corruption: for of whom a man is overcome, of the same is he brought in bondage."

— 2 Peter 2:19 (KJV)

Repeated exposure trains responses. Over time:

- shock fades

- resistance weakens

- conscience dulls

What once felt wrong begins to feel normal.

This is not accidental—it is how influence works.

Desensitization Removes Restraint

Scripture warns about a dangerous condition of the heart:

"Who being past feeling have given themselves over unto lasciviousness, to work all uncleanness with greediness."

— Ephesians 4:19 (KJV)

To be **"past feeling"** means sensitivity has been lost. Repeated exposure to sin dulls conviction. When limitation is removed, **impulse takes over.**

Desensitization does not mean a person becomes evil overnight.

It means the **inner alarms stop sounding.**

The Slow Drift of Agreement

Agreement does not usually come through one bold decision. It comes through small, repeated allowances.

Scripture describes this progression:

"But exhort one another daily… lest any of you be hardened through the deceitfulness of sin."

— Hebrews 3:13 (KJV)

Sin is deceitful because it convinces people that repetition has no cost. Over time, the heart agrees with what it is repeatedly exposed to.

James explains it clearly:

"Every man is tempted, when he is drawn away of his own lust, and enticed.

Then when lust hath conceived, it bringeth forth sin..."

— James 1:14–15 (KJV)

Agreement happens before action.

Why Youth Are Especially Vulnerable

Youth are not weak—they are **unfinished.**

Scripture acknowledges the need for early instruction:

"Train up a child in the way he should go."

— Proverbs 22:6 (KJV)

When training is missing, repetition fills the gap. Without guidance, repetition becomes instruction. Without correction, exposure becomes permission.

That is why youth are targeted—because **habits formed early are harder to break later.**

Interrupting the Pattern

The Bible does not leave people trapped in cycles. It offers a way to interrupt repetition.

"Be not conformed to this world: but be ye transformed by the renewing of your mind."

— Romans 12:2 (KJV)

Renewal requires **replacement.** What is removed must be replaced with truth. What is repeated must be countered with wisdom.

Scripture calls this discipline:

"Exercise thyself rather unto godliness."

— 1 Timothy 4:7 (KJV)

Repetition can enslave—but it can also rehabilitate.

A Different Drift Is Possible

Just as repetition can lead toward destruction, it can also lead toward wisdom.

"His delight is in the law of the LORD; and in his law doth he meditate day and night."

— Psalm 1:2 (KJV)

What a person dwells on shapes where they drift.

The same process that trained wrong thinking can be used to retrain right thinking—when direction changes.

Closing Charge

You did not become who you are overnight.

And you will not change overnight.

But the same repetition that shaped your past can shape a different future—if it is interrupted with truth.

"Stand fast therefore in the liberty wherewith Christ hath made us free."
— **Galatians 5:1 (KJV)**

Freedom begins with awareness—and continues with discipline.

Reflective Summary

Scripture teaches that repetition shapes the heart and that desensitization removes limitation **(Ephesians 4:19; Hebrews 3:13).**

Youth are especially vulnerable when instruction is missing and repetition becomes the primary teacher. Sin works gradually, through agreement formed over time **(James 1:14–15).**

God offers renewal by replacing harmful repetition with disciplined truth **(Romans 12:2).**

Reflective Questions

1. What behaviors or thoughts became normal to me through repetition? **(Hebrews 3:13)**

2. Can I identify moments when something that once felt wrong stopped bothering me? **(Ephesians 4:19)**

3. What patterns of repetition shaped my thinking before my actions changed? **(James 1:14–15)**

4. What truths or disciplines could interrupt unhealthy patterns in my life now? **(Romans 12:2)**

5. Am I willing to be patient with the process of retraining my mind? **(1 Timothy 4:7)**

Prayer

Lord,

I recognize that repetition shaped much of my thinking and behavior. I ask You to help me break harmful patterns and to renew my mind with truth.

Restore sensitivity where it has been dulled, and give me discipline to replace what leads to destruction with what leads to life.

Guide me patiently as You reshape my heart and direction.

In Jesus' Name, Amen.

CHAPTER 6

IDENTITY, BELONGING, AND THE SEARCH FOR WORTH

"As a man thinketh in his heart, so is he."

— Proverbs 23:7 (KJV)

Every young person is searching for the same thing—**identity.**

Long before choices are made, before paths are chosen, before consequences appear, a quiet question is being asked in the heart: **Who am I?**

Closely connected to that question is another:
Where do I belong?

When those questions go unanswered by parents, mentors, and truth, **someone else will answer them.**

Scripture teaches that identity does not form in isolation. It is shaped by what a person believes about themselves, what they are told they are worth, and where they are accepted.

Identity Is Formed Before Behavior

The Bible makes it clear that behavior flows from belief.

"For as he thinketh in his heart, so is he."

— Proverbs 23:7 (KJV)

A young person does not wake up one day and suddenly act out. Long before action, identity has already been forming. Thoughts become beliefs, beliefs become labels, and labels become behavior.

This is why Scripture warns against accepting false definitions:

"Thus saith the LORD, Let not the wise man glory in his wisdom, neither let the mighty man glory in his might, let not the rich man glory in his riches."

— Jeremiah 9:23 (KJV)

False identities always promise worth—but never deliver peace.

Belonging Is a Powerful Force

God created people to belong.

"It is not good that the man should be alone."

— Genesis 2:18 (KJV)

When healthy belonging is absent, unhealthy belonging fills the gap. Youth often attach themselves to **groups, movements,** or **cultures** not because they love the behavior—but because they crave acceptance.

Scripture warns about this pull:

"He that walketh with wise men shall be wise: but a companion of fools shall be destroyed."

— Proverbs 13:20 (KJV)

Association shape's identity. Over time, belonging teaches a person who they are allowed to be.

False Identity Is Often Offered First

When godly instruction is missing, the world steps in quickly with substitutes.

Industries and environments often offer:

- status through violence

- respect through fear

- worth through attention

- belonging through rebellion

Scripture calls this deception:

"There is a way which seemeth right unto a man, but the end thereof are the ways of death."

— Proverbs 14:12 (KJV)

These identities feel empowering at first—but they always demand a price.

Labels Become Lived Reality

What a person is repeatedly called—or calls themselves—becomes internalized.

Scripture warns:

"Thou shalt not bear false witness against thy neighbour."

— Exodus 20:16 (KJV)

False witness includes lies spoken about oneself.

When youth accept labels like:

- "troublemaker"

- "gang member"

- "nobody"

- "lost cause"

those words shape expectation and behavior.

Jesus said:

"If ye continue in my word... ye shall know the truth, and the truth shall make you free."

— **John 8:31–32 (KJV)**

Truth breaks false identity.

God's Definition Comes First

God does not wait for behavior to define worth.

"Before I formed thee in the belly I knew thee."

— Jeremiah 1:5 (KJV)

Identity, in Scripture, begins with **being known by God,** not approved by people.

Peter reminds believers:

"Ye are a chosen generation, a royal priesthood, an holy nation, a peculiar people."

— 1 Peter 2:9 (KJV)

God's identity is not earned—it is **revealed.**

Why This Matters for Your Life

Many incarcerated youths were searching for worth in places that offered acceptance without instruction. They found belonging—but not **guidance.** Identity—**but not truth.**

That does not mean they were weak.

It means they were **hungry.**

Scripture explains this hunger:

"Blessed are they which do hunger and thirst after righteousness."

— Matthew 5:6 (KJV)

Hunger itself is not the problem. **What feeds it is.**

Learning to Belong Without Losing Yourself

God does not remove the need for belonging—He redirects it.

"God setteth the solitary in families."

— Psalm 68:6 (KJV)

True belonging does not require **destruction, silence,** or **compromise.** It strengthens identity instead of replacing it.

Closing Charge

You are more than the labels you were given or accepted.

You may have been searching for worth in places that did not care about you—but God does.

"Fear thou not; for I am with thee… I will help thee."

— Isaiah 41:10 (KJV)

Your identity is not lost. It can be reclaimed.

Reflective Summary

Scripture teaches that identity forms before behavior **(Proverbs 23:7)** and that belonging powerfully shapes direction **(Proverbs 13:20).**

When godly instruction is missing, false identities are offered that promise worth but lead to destruction **(Proverbs 14:12).**

God defines identity based on His knowledge and purpose, not past behavior **(Jeremiah 1:5; 1 Peter 2:9).** True belonging restores identity rather than replacing it.

Reflective Questions

1. What labels have I accepted about myself that may not align with God's truth? **(John 8:31–32)**

2. Where did I first feel a sense of belonging, and what did it require of me? **(Proverbs 13:20)**

3. Can I see how my search for worth influenced my choices? **(Proverbs 23:7)**

4. What does Scripture say about who I am apart from my past actions? **(1 Peter 2:9)**

5. What kind of belonging would help me grow instead of destroy me? **(Psalm 68:6)**

Prayer

Lord,

I confess that I have searched for worth and belonging in places that did not lead me toward life.

Help me to see myself through Your truth, not through labels or past mistakes.

Replace false identity with understanding, and guide me toward belonging that strengthens rather than destroys.

Teach me who I am in You and help me walk in that truth.

In Jesus' Name, Amen.

CHAPTER 7

ANGER, RETALIATION, AND THE CULTURE OF RESPONSE

"Be not hasty in thy spirit to be angry: for anger resteth in the bosom of fools."

— Ecclesiastes 7:9 (KJV)

Anger is not condemned in Scripture.

Living in anger is.

Scripture acknowledges anger as a real human emotion, but it warns repeatedly about what happens when anger is **uncontrolled, justified, or rehearsed.**

For many youth, anger was not something they learned to manage—it was something they learned to **express immediately,** often through retaliation.

Before violence becomes an action, it becomes a **response pattern.**

Anger that is never processed does not disappear. It settles. And what settles eventually governs.

Anger Is Often Learned, Not Chosen

The Bible teaches that responses are shaped long before they are expressed.

"He that is slow to wrath is of great understanding: but he that is hasty of spirit exalteth folly."

— Proverbs 14:29 (KJV)

Many young people were raised in environments where anger was **modeled, rewarded,** or **necessary for survival.** Calm responses were interpreted as weakness. Restraint was mistaken for fear. Retaliation was presented as respect.

This does not mean anger itself was evil.

It means **anger was trained without wisdom.**

When anger becomes the default response,
discernment is crowded out.

The Culture of Retaliation

Scripture warns against reflexive response:

"Say not thou, I will recompense evil; but wait on the LORD."

— Proverbs 20:22 (KJV)

Yet many youths were taught—directly or indirectly—that retaliation was required to maintain identity, safety, or status. Disrespect demanded a response. Silence invited escalation.

Over time, retaliation stopped feeling optional and started feeling **necessary.**

The Bible describes this danger clearly:

"An angry man stirreth up strife, and a furious man aboundeth in transgression."

— Proverbs 29:22 (KJV)

What begins as a response often ends as multiplied consequences.

Anger That Is Fed Becomes Control

Unmanaged anger does not stay emotional—it becomes **controlling.**

"He that hath no rule over his own spirit is like a city that is broken down, and without walls."

— Proverbs 25:28 (KJV)

When anger governs response, discernment disappears. Decisions are made quickly. Words are spoken carelessly. Actions escalate. Consequences follow relentlessly.

This is why Scripture connects anger to bondage and association:

"Make no friendship with an angry man; and with a furious man thou shalt not go."

— Proverbs 22:24 (KJV)

Anger spreads. It trains others how to respond. What is tolerated long enough is eventually imitated.

Retaliation Feels Powerful—but It Is Costly

Retaliation promises control, respect, and relief.

But Scripture reveals the cost:

"Wrath is cruel, and anger is outrageous; but who is able to stand before envy?"

— Proverbs 27:4 (KJV)

Many people did not intend to go as far as they did. They intended to respond—not to destroy. But anger narrows vision and silences wisdom.

James explains the outcome:

"For the wrath of man worketh not the righteousness of God."

— James 1:20 (KJV)

Anger may feel justified, but it rarely produces the outcome hoped for.

Jesus and a Different Response

Jesus directly addressed retaliation:

"Ye have heard that it hath been said... But I say unto you..."

— Matthew 5:38–39 (KJV)

Jesus did not deny injustice or pain. He challenged **reflexive response.** He offered restraint—not as weakness, but as **strength under control.**

Scripture defines this strength:

"Better is he that ruleth his spirit than he that taketh a city."

— **Proverbs 16:32 (KJV)**

Self-control is power.

Why This Matters for Your Life

Many incarcerated youths were not violent because they wanted chaos—they were violent because anger had become their **default language.** Retaliation felt automatic. Pausing felt dangerous.

That does not excuse the harm done.

But it explains **how reactions were trained.**

God offers a different way:

"Let all bitterness, and wrath, and anger… be put away from you."

— Ephesians 4:31 (KJV)

Putting something away requires **replacement, not denial.**

Learning a New Response

The Bible does not command people to stop feeling—it teaches them to **respond wisely.**

"A soft answer turneth away wrath: but grievous words stir up anger."

— Proverbs 15:1 (KJV)

Anger can be acknowledged without being obeyed.

A new response can be trained.

Closing Charge

Anger does not have to control you.

You may have been trained to respond quickly, but you can learn to respond wisely.

"He that is slow to anger is better than the mighty."

— Proverbs 16:32 (KJV)

Strength is not found in retaliation—but in restraint.

Reflective Summary

Scripture teaches that anger is real but dangerous when unrestrained **(Proverbs 14:29).** Many youths were trained in cultures where retaliation was normalized and silence was seen as weakness.

Unmanaged anger leads to loss of control and multiplied consequences **(Proverbs 29:22; James 1:20).**

God offers a different response—**self-control, patience,** and **wisdom**—which Scripture defines as greater strength than violence.

Reflective Questions

1. How was anger modeled or handled in the environment I grew up in? **(Proverbs 14:29)**

2. Can I see how retaliation became my default response? **(Proverbs 20:22)**

3. What situations trigger my anger most quickly? **(James 1:20)**

4. What does Scripture say about strength and self-control? **(Proverbs 16:32)**

5. What new response could I begin training when anger rises? **(Proverbs 15:1)**

Prayer

Lord,

You know my anger and the reasons behind it.

I ask You to help me slow down, gain understanding, and respond with wisdom instead of impulse.

Teach me to rule my spirit and to choose restraint over retaliation.

Heal what has fueled my anger and guide me toward responses that lead to peace and life.

In Jesus' Name, Amen.

CHAPTER 8

CONSEQUENCES, ACCOUNTABILITY, AND WHEN REALITY ARRIVES

"Be not deceived; God is not mocked: for whatsoever a man soweth, that shall he also reap."

— Galatians 6:7 (KJV)

Every pattern eventually produces an outcome.

Scripture teaches that consequences are not accidents—they are **arrivals.** What is repeatedly thought, spoken, and acted upon eventually shows up in real life.

For many youths, the shock was not that consequences came, but **how fast and how final they felt.**

Before a sentence is handed down, before a door closes, before freedom is lost, a path has already been walked.

Consequences Are Connected, Not Random

The Bible makes this principle unmistakably clear:

"He that soweth iniquity shall reap vanity."

— Proverbs 22:8 (KJV)

Consequences are connected to patterns. What entered through the gates, what was rehearsed in the heart, what was justified in speech, and what was acted upon in anger eventually reached a point where reality could no longer be postponed.

This is not cruelty—it is truth.

Accountability Is Not Condemnation

Many youths hear the word accountability and think punishment. Scripture presents accountability differently.

"Every one of us shall give account of himself to God."

— Romans 14:12 (KJV)

Accountability is about **ownership,** not shame. It is the moment a person stops blaming environment, people, or circumstances and begins to see how choices—trained or untrained—produced outcomes.

This does not deny influence.

It recognizes responsibility **after influence.**

When Reality Arrives

Reality arrives when excuses run out.

"The way of the transgressor is hard."

— Proverbs 13:15 (KJV)

Many youths did not believe consequences
would come this far or this fast. They believed:

- I'll deal with it later

- I won't get caught

- It won't happen to me

But Scripture warns:

*"Because sentence against an evil work is not
executed speedily, therefore the heart of the sons
of men is fully set in them to do evil."*

— Ecclesiastes 8:11 (KJV)

Delay is not permission.

The Moment of Clarity

For many incarcerated youth, confinement brought the first moment of clarity—time to think, time to reflect, time without noise.

Scripture speaks to this moment:

"I thought on my ways, and turned my feet unto thy testimonies."

— Psalm 119:59 (KJV)

Consequences can become teachers if pride does not silence the lesson.

Responsibility Without Hopelessness

Scripture never presents consequences as the end of the story.

"Though he fall, he shall not be utterly cast down: for the LORD upholdeth him with his hand."

— Psalm 37:24 (KJV)

God does not deny the reality of consequences— but He does not abandon those who face them honestly.

Ownership opens the door to change.

Correction Is an Act of Care

The Bible reframes correction:

"For whom the LORD loveth he correcteth."

— Proverbs 3:12 (KJV)

Correction is not rejection. It is intervention before destruction goes further.

What You Do After Reality Arrives Matters Most

The most important decision is not the one that led here—it is the one made now.

"Today if ye will hear his voice, harden not your hearts."

— Hebrews 3:15 (KJV)

The past explains where you are.

It does not decide where you go next.

Closing Charge

Consequences are real—but they are not final unless you refuse to learn.

Reality has arrived, but so has opportunity.

"It is good for me that I have been afflicted; that I might learn thy statutes."

— Psalm 119:71 (KJV)

What you learn here can redirect your future.

Reflective Summary

Scripture teaches that consequences follow patterns and choices **(Galatians 6:7).**

Accountability is not condemnation but ownership **(Romans 14:12).**

Though reality arrives with force, God does not abandon those who respond with humility and honesty **(Psalm 37:24).**

Correction can become a turning point when it is received with understanding.

Reflective Questions

1. What patterns led me to this moment? **(Galatians 6:7)**

2. Where did I ignore warnings or delay responsibility? (Ecclesiastes 8:11)

3. What has this season taught me about myself and my choices? **(Psalm 119:59)**

4. How does Scripture define accountability differently than punishment? **(Romans 14:12)**

5. What decision can I make now that would begin changing my direction? **(Hebrews 3:15)**

Prayer

Lord,

I acknowledge the reality of where my choices have led me.

I ask You for humility to learn, courage to take responsibility, and wisdom to choose differently moving forward.

Do not let this season be wasted. Use it to shape my heart, correct my path, and guide me toward a future marked by understanding and hope.

In Jesus name, Amen.

CHAPTER 9

RENEWAL, RETRAINING THE MIND, AND THE POSSIBILITY OF CHANGE

"And be not conformed to this world: but be ye transformed by the renewing of your mind."

— Romans 12:2 (KJV)

Renewal is not optional in a world that trains the mind daily.

Scripture teaches that just as the mind can be shaped toward destruction, it can also be **retrained toward life.** Renewal does not deny the past—it **interrupts its influence.**

God does not ask a person to pretend they were not influenced; He calls them to understand how influence works and to choose differently moving forward.

Today's challenge is not subtle influence. It is **constant saturation.**

From Subliminal Influence to Open Indoctrination

In the past, influence often worked quietly—suggesting ideas beneath awareness. Today, the messages shaping youth are **not hidden.** They are direct, repeated, and unapologetic.

Violence is celebrated.

Sexual immorality is normalized.

Disrespect is marketed as confidence.

Lawlessness is framed as authenticity.

Scripture warned of this shift:

"Woe unto them that call evil good, and good evil."

— Isaiah 5:20 (KJV)

What was once whispered is now broadcast. What was once questioned is now rewarded.

This means renewal must be **intentional,** not passive.

Renewal Is a Process, Not a Moment

The Bible never presents transformation as instant.

"Though our outward man perish, yet the inward man is renewed day by day."

— 2 Corinthians 4:16 (KJV)

The same repetition that trained the mind toward anger, impulse, and retaliation must now be replaced with repetition toward **truth, wisdom, and restraint.**

Renewal is daily resistance to saturation.

Retraining the Mind Requires Replacement

Scripture does not say stop thinking—it says think differently.

"Finally, brethren, whatsoever things are true... think on these things."

— Philippians 4:8 (KJV)

The mind cannot remain empty. What is removed must be **replaced.** Old patterns are not broken by silence but by **truth** crowding out deception.

This is why Scripture teaches:

"As a man thinketh in his heart, so is he."

— **Proverbs 23:7 (KJV)**

Thoughts shape **identity.** Identity shapes **choices.**

Strong Messages Create Strong Agreement

Repetition creates familiarity. Familiarity creates agreement. Agreement creates direction.

The Bible warns:

"Evil communications corrupt good manners."

— 1 Corinthians 15:33 (KJV)

Corruption today does not require secrecy—only exposure. When messages are seen, heard, repeated, and celebrated, they become normal. When they become normal, resistance weakens.

This is why Jesus said:

"Take heed what ye hear."

— **Mark 4:24 (KJV)**

Not because messages are hidden—but because they are formative.

Guarding the Gates in a Loud World

Renewal requires returning to the gates with understanding.

"Keep thy heart with all diligence; for out of it are the issues of life."

— **Proverbs 4:23 (KJV)**

- What you **see** trains imagination

- What you **hear** shapes belief

- What you **repeat** reinforces identity

In a world that shouts constantly, discernment becomes survival.

Hope That Is Grounded, Not Imagined

Many youth feel overwhelmed by the strength of the messages around them. Scripture does not deny the pressure—it offers power to resist it.

"Where sin abounded, grace did much more abound."

— Romans 5:20 (KJV)

Grace does not remove **responsibility**—it provides strength to change direction.

Why This Matters for Your Life

You were influenced—but you are not trapped.

Scripture promises:

"If any man be in Christ, he is a new creature: old things are passed away; behold, all things are become new."

— 2 Corinthians 5:17 (KJV)

New does not mean untouched.

It means **retrained.**

Closing Charge

You cannot control the volume of the world—but you can choose which voice you agree with.

Renewal begins when you decide that saturation will no longer decide your direction.

"Commit thy works unto the LORD, and thy thoughts shall be established."

— Proverbs 16:3 (KJV)

Change is not accidental.

It is intentional.

Reflective Summary

Scripture teaches that renewal requires resisting conformity in a world that openly promotes destructive values **(Romans 12:2; Isaiah 5:20).**

Modern influence is not subliminal but saturating, making intentional replacement and gate-guarding essential.

Transformation is a daily process of retraining the mind through *truth, discipline,* and *discernment* **(Philippians 4:8; Proverbs 4:23).**

Reflective Questions

1. What messages have I been repeatedly exposed to that shaped my thinking? **(1 Corinthians 15:33)**

2. How have constant messages made certain behaviors feel normal? **(Isaiah 5:20)**

3. What thoughts do I need to begin replacing with truth? **(Philippians 4:8)**

4. Which gate—eyes, ears, or mouth—needs the most attention right now? **(Proverbs 4:23)**

5. What would resisting saturation look like for me today? **(Romans 12:2)**

Prayer

Lord,

I recognize how much influence has surrounded me and shaped my thinking.

I ask You to help me renew my mind and resist the messages that lead away from life.

Teach me discernment, discipline, and wisdom.

Help me guard my **eyes, ears,** and **words** so that truth can take root in my heart.

I believe You can retrain what was misdirected and lead me forward.

In Jesus name, Amen.

CHAPTER 10

WISDOM, COUNSEL, AND CHOOSING THE RIGHT VOICES

"Where no counsel is, the people fall: but in the multitude of counsellors there is safety."

— **Proverbs 11:14 (KJV)**

No one is shaped in isolation.

Scripture teaches that voices guide direction. Every life is influenced by counsel—whether it is wise or reckless, intentional or accidental.

The question is not whether you are being instructed, but **who is instructing you.**

In a world filled with noise, choosing the right voices becomes a matter of survival.

Every Life Is Being Counseled

Many youths believe they acted on their own. Scripture says otherwise.

"Hear counsel, and receive instruction, that thou mayest be wise in thy latter end."

— Proverbs 19:20 (KJV)

Music counsels.

Peers counsel.

Social media counsels.

Street culture counsels.

Even silence counsels when wisdom is absent.

If a person does not choose counsel, counsel will still be chosen for them.

Bad Counsel Feels Familiar

Wrong voices often sound right because they are familiar.

"There is a way which seemeth right unto a man, but the end thereof are the ways of death."

— Proverbs 14:12 (KJV)

Familiarity breeds comfort, not correctness. Many youth trusted voices that affirmed anger, justified retaliation, normalized lawlessness, and rewarded impulse.

Scripture warns:

"The simple believeth every word: but the prudent man looketh well to his going."

— Proverbs 14:15 (KJV)

Wisdom questions voices instead of assuming they are safe.

The Power of Agreement

Counsel shapes agreement, and agreement shapes direction.

"Can two walk together, except they be agreed?"

— Amos 3:3 (KJV)

Agreement does not require a contract. It requires **repetition and trust.** When a voice is heard long enough, it begins to feel reasonable. When it feels reasonable, it is followed.

This is why Scripture warns:

"My son, if sinners entice thee, consent thou not."

— Proverbs 1:10 (KJV)

Consent begins in the mind—long before action follows.

Wisdom Is Not Loud, but It Is Steady

The loudest voices are not always the wisest.

"Wisdom crieth without; she uttereth her voice in the streets."

— Proverbs 1:20 (KJV)

Wisdom speaks consistently, not impulsively. It calls for restraint when emotion demands reaction. It calls for patience when pressure demands speed.

James describes wisdom clearly:

*"The wisdom that is from above is first pure,
then peaceable, gentle, and easy to be intreated."*

— James 3:17 (KJV)

Wisdom does not push—**it guides.**

Learning to Trust New Voices

For many youths, the hardest part of change is trusting voices that challenge old habits.

Scripture encourages this shift:

"He that walketh with wise men shall be wise: but a companion of fools shall be destroyed."

— Proverbs 13:20 (KJV)

Walking with the wise does not mean instant perfection. It means **gradual correction.**

Growth happens through exposure to voices that:

- tell the truth

- challenge impulsive thinking

- promote accountability

- encourage restraint

God's Voice Above All Others

Above every counselor stands **God** Himself.

"Trust in the LORD with all thine heart; and lean not unto thine own understanding."

— **Proverbs 3:5 (KJV)**

God's voice does not compete—it clarifies.

"Thy word is a lamp unto my feet, and a light unto my path."

— **Psalm 119:105 (KJV)**

A lamp does not show the whole journey—it shows **the next step.**

Why This Matters for Your Life

Many incarcerated youths followed voices that never intended to stay for the consequences. **Wisdom** stays. **Truth** stays. **God** stays.

Scripture promises:

"I will instruct thee and teach thee in the way which thou shalt go."

— Psalm 32:8 (KJV)

Guidance is available—but it must be received.

Closing Charge

The voices you follow today will determine the direction you walk tomorrow.

Choose counsel that leads to life, not applause.

"Incline thine ear unto wisdom, and apply thine heart to understanding."

— Proverbs 2:2 (KJV)

Wisdom is not inherited.

It is chosen.

Reflective Summary

Scripture teaches that counsel shapes direction and agreement precede action **(Proverbs 11:14; Amos 3:3).** In a noisy world, wisdom requires discernment and intentional listening.

Wrong voices often feel right because they are **familiar,** but godly counsel produces peace, restraint, and life **(James 3:17).** Choosing the right voices is essential for lasting change.

Reflective Questions

1. Who or what has influenced my decisions the most? **(Proverbs 19:20)**

2. Which voices have justified behaviors that led to harm? **(Proverbs 14:12)**

3. What does Scripture say about the kind of counsel that leads to wisdom? **(James 3:17)**

4. Who are some wise voices I could begin listening to now? **(Proverbs 13:20)**

5. How can I make God's Word a daily guide for my decisions? **(Psalm 119:105)**

Prayer

Lord,

Help me recognize which voices have shaped my thinking and where I need new instruction.

Give me humility to receive correction and discernment to choose wisdom over familiarity.

Teach me to trust Your Word above every other voice and guide my steps one decision at a time.

In Jesus name, Amen.

CHAPTER 11

RESPONSIBILITY, OBEDIENCE, AND LIVING WITH INTENTION

"To him that knoweth to do good, and doeth it not, to him it is sin."

— James 4:17 (KJV)

Awareness changes responsibility.

Once a person understands how influence
works—how thoughts are trained, how responses
are learned, how paths are formed—life can no
longer be lived on autopilot.

Scripture teaches that knowledge brings
accountability, not condemnation. Obedience is
no longer accidental; it becomes **intentional.**

This chapter is about crossing that line—from
reaction to responsibility, from impulse to
intention.

Responsibility Begins With Ownership

The Bible never denies outside influence, but it consistently calls individuals to ownership **after understanding.**

"So then every one of us shall give account of himself to God."

— Romans 14:12 (KJV)

Ownership does not mean denying what shaped you.

It means refusing to let it excuse you forever.

Many youths were trained in environments that rewarded **impulse** and punished restraint.

Scripture acknowledges that—but it also teaches that a turning point comes when a person says, **"This ends with me."**

Obedience Is Alignment, Not Control

Obedience is often misunderstood as restriction. Scripture presents it as **alignment.**

"If ye be willing and obedient, ye shall eat the good of the land."

— Isaiah 1:19 (KJV)

Obedience aligns behavior with truth. It is not about perfection—it is about **direction.**

When a person chooses obedience, they are choosing to move with God instead of against reality.

Jesus made this clear:

"If ye love me, keep my commandments."
— **John 14:15 (KJV)**

Obedience is evidence of trust.

Living With Intention Means Choosing Before Pressure

Many failures happen not because a person wanted destruction, but because they never decided **ahead of time.**

Scripture teaches pre-decision:

"I have set the LORD always before me."

— Psalm 16:8 (KJV)

Living with intention means deciding:

- what you will allow

- what you will refuse

- how you will respond

- who you will walk with

Before pressure arrives.

Discipline Trains Intention

Intentional living requires discipline—not punishment, but training.

"For God hath not given us the spirit of fear; but of power, and of love, and of a sound mind."

— 2 Timothy 1:7 (KJV)

A sound mind is **a trained mind.** Discipline reinforces what intention decides.

Paul describes this clearly:

"I keep under my body, and bring it into subjection."

— 1 Corinthians 9:27 (KJV)

Self-governance is strength.

Small Choices Shape Large Outcomes

Scripture consistently emphasizes the power of small decisions.

"He that is faithful in that which is least is faithful also in much."

— Luke 16:10 (KJV)

Intentional living is not dramatic. It is daily. Quiet obedience, repeated over time, reshapes character and redirects outcomes.

Why This Matters for Your Life

Many youths regret a single moment. Scripture teaches that moments are usually the result of **patterns.**

Living with intention breaks those patterns.

"Order my steps in thy word: and let not any iniquity have dominion over me."

— Psalm 119:133 (KJV)

Dominion shifts when obedience becomes **consistent.**

Closing Charge

You cannot change yesterday, but you can govern today.

Responsibility is not a burden—it is freedom when guided by wisdom.

"Choose you this day whom ye will serve."
— Joshua 24:15 (KJV)

Live on purpose. Decide before pressure.

Reflective Summary

Scripture teaches that awareness brings responsibility and that obedience is alignment with truth, not restriction **(James 4:17; Isaiah 1:19).**

Living with intention requires ownership, pre-decision, and discipline.

Small, consistent choices reshape direction and prevent past patterns from controlling the future **(Luke 16:10).**

Reflective Questions

1. What responsibilities do I now recognize that I once ignored? **(James 4:17)**

2. How have my past choices been driven more by **reaction** than intention? **(Psalm 16:8)**

3. What does Scripture say about obedience and trust? **(John 14:15)**

4. What small daily **decision** could help me live more intentionally? **(Luke 16:10)**

5. How can I prepare for pressure before it arrives? **(Psalm 119:133)**

Prayer

Lord,

I accept responsibility for my choices and ask You to help me live with intention.

Teach me obedience that aligns my life with Your truth.

Give me discipline, clarity, and strength to choose wisely before pressure rises.

Order my steps and guide my decisions so that my future reflects **understanding, growth**, and **purpose.**

In Jesus name, Amen.

CHAPTER 12

HOPE, RESTORATION, AND FINISHING STRONG

"Being confident of this very thing, that he which hath begun a good work in you will perform it until the day of Jesus Christ."

— Philippians 1:6 (KJV)

Hope is not denial of reality—it is confidence in God's ability to restore what has been broken.

Scripture never pretends that damage did not happen. It speaks honestly about failure, loss, and consequence. Yet it consistently points beyond them to **restoration.**

God does not abandon a life because it took a wrong path. He meets people **at the point of truth** and offers a new direction forward.

Finishing strong is not about where you started or where you fell—it is about **how you walk from here.**

Restoration Begins With Truth

The Bible does not offer restoration without honesty.

"If we confess our sins, he is faithful and just to forgive us our sins, and to cleanse us from all unrighteousness."

— 1 John 1:9 (KJV)

Confession is not humiliation—**it is alignment.** When truth is acknowledged, healing can begin. God does not restore what is hidden.

He restores what is **brought into the light.**

"He that covereth his sins shall not prosper: but whoso confesseth and forsaketh them shall have mercy."

— Proverbs 28:13 (KJV)

Mercy follows honesty.

God Restores What Was Misused

Many youth believe they wasted their life, their time, or their potential. Scripture says otherwise.

"And I will restore to you the years that the locust hath eaten."

— Joel 2:25 (KJV)

Restoration does not rewind the clock—but it **redeems the remainder.** God is able to take what was misdirected and give it **purpose.**

"All things work together for good to them that love God."

— Romans 8:28 (KJV)

Even consequences can become classrooms.

Hope Is Anchored, Not Imagined

Biblical hope is not wishful thinking. It is anchored expectation.

"Which hope we have as an anchor of the soul, both sure and stedfast."

— Hebrews 6:19 (KJV)

Hope holds when emotions fluctuate and circumstances resist change. It steadies a person long enough for **transformation** to take root.

Finishing Strong Requires Endurance

The Bible emphasizes endurance over speed.

"Let us run with patience the race that is set before us."

— Hebrews 12:1 (KJV)

Many people start strong and finish weak. Scripture calls believers to the opposite—**steady faithfulness over time.**

"He that endureth to the end shall be saved."

— Matthew 24:13 (KJV)

Endurance is faith practiced **daily.**

Your Past Does Not Have the Final Word

Scripture repeatedly shows God using people with complicated histories.

"Brethren, I count not myself to have apprehended: but this one thing I do, forgetting those things which are behind, and reaching forth unto those things which are before."

— Philippians 3:13 (KJV)

Forgetting does not mean ignoring. It means refusing to live **backward.**

Walking Forward With Purpose

God does not restore people simply to survive—but to live **purposefully.**

"For we are his workmanship, created in Christ Jesus unto good works."

— Ephesians 2:10 (KJV)

Your life has **value** beyond your past mistakes. Purpose emerges when **obedience, wisdom,** and **endurance** walk together.

Closing Charge

You are not finished.

God is still working, still shaping, still restoring.

"The steps of a good man are ordered by the LORD."

— Psalm 37:23 (KJV)

Finish strong. Walk forward with hope.

Reflective Summary

Scripture teaches that hope is grounded in God's **faithfulness,** restoration follows truth, and endurance leads to completion **(Philippians 1:6; 1 John 1:9).**

God is able to redeem lost time and redirect broken paths. Finishing strong requires **honesty, patience,** and **trust** that God's work is ongoing.

Reflective Questions

1. What does Scripture teach about God's commitment to finishing His work in me? **(Philippians 1:6)**

2. How does honesty open the door to restoration? **(1 John 1:9)**

3. In what ways could God redeem what I believe was wasted? **(Joel 2:25)**

4. What does enduring faith look like in my daily life? **(Hebrews 12:1)**

5. What step forward can I take today instead of looking backward? **(Philippians 3:13)**

Prayer

Lord,

I thank You that my life is not over and my story is not finished.

Help me walk forward in **truth, endurance,** and **hope.**

Restore what has been broken, redeem what has been misused, and guide me toward the purpose You designed for me.

Strengthen me to finish well, trusting You each step of the way.

In Jesus' name, Amen.

A FINAL CHARGE: GUARD WHAT GOD IS REBUILDING

You have been shown how influence works.

You have been given language for what shaped you.

You have seen that your life is not random, forgotten, or finished.

Now the responsibility is yours.

Scripture teaches that understanding changes obligation:

"To whom much is given, of him shall be much required." **(Luke 12:48)**

This is not condemnation.

It is an invitation to live awake.

Guard your eyes.

Guard your ears.

Guard your mouth.

Guard your heart.

The world will not stop shouting—but you do not have to agree with it.

"Keep thy heart with all diligence; for out of it are the issues of life." **(Proverbs 4:23)**

You may not control where you are today, but you can control **what you allow to shape you tomorrow.**

God is not finished with you.

But what He is rebuilding must be protected.

Choose wisdom.

Choose restraint.

Choose truth.

And when you stumble—get up and walk
forward again.

SCRIPTURES TO KEEP CLOSE

These Scriptures were chosen to help you guard your mind, steady your heart, and walk forward with wisdom. Return to them often. Read them slowly. Let them speak.

Guarding the Heart & Mind

"Keep thy heart with all diligence; for out of it are the issues of life."

— Proverbs 4:23 (KJV)

"As a man thinketh in his heart, so is he."

— Proverbs 23:7 (KJV)

"Set a watch, O LORD, before my mouth; keep the door of my lips."

— Psalm 141:3 (KJV)

Wisdom & Discernment

"If any of you lack wisdom, let him ask of God."

— James 1:5 (KJV)

"The fear of the LORD is the beginning of wisdom."

— Proverbs 9:10 (KJV)

"Hear counsel, and receive instruction, that thou mayest be wise in thy latter end."

— Proverbs 19:20 (KJV)

Anger, Self-Control & Restraint

"Be not hasty in thy spirit to be angry."

— Ecclesiastes 7:9 (KJV)

"He that is slow to anger is better than the mighty."

— Proverbs 16:32 (KJV)

"The wrath of man worketh not the righteousness of God."

— James 1:20 (KJV)

Renewal & Change

"Be ye transformed by the renewing of your mind."

— **Romans 12:2 (KJV)**

"If any man be in Christ, he is a new creature."

— **2 Corinthians 5:17 (KJV)**

"Create in me a clean heart, O God."

— **Psalm 51:10 (KJV)**

Responsibility & Direction

"Choose you this day whom ye will serve."

— Joshua 24:15 (KJV)

"Commit thy works unto the LORD, and thy thoughts shall be established."

— Proverbs 16:3 (KJV)

"Order my steps in thy word."

— Psalm 119:133 (KJV)

Hope & Endurance

"For I know the thoughts that I think toward you... to give you an expected end."

— Jeremiah 29:11 (KJV)

"Let us run with patience the race that is set before us."

— Hebrews 12:1 (KJV)

"He which hath begun a good work in you will perform it."

— Philippians 1:6 (KJV)

A Final Scripture to Hold Onto

"The LORD shall preserve thy going out and thy coming in from this time forth, and even for evermore."

— Psalm 121:8 (KJV)

AUTHOR'S CLOSING WORD

I wrote this book because too many young people have been blamed for outcomes without anyone ever explaining how **influence works.**

Long before choices were made, minds were being trained, responses were being shaped, and paths were being set—often by voices and systems that offered no guidance, no protection, and no concern for the aftermath.

This book was not written to excuse wrongdoing.

It was written to **explain, to clarify,** and to **call you forward.**

You are more than your worst decision.

You are more than the moment that brought you here.

And your future does not have to repeat your past.

If this book helped you see yourself more clearly, guard your mind more carefully, or pause before reacting, then it has done its work. Growth does not happen all at once—it happens one decision at a time, practiced daily, often quietly.

Wherever you are reading this from, know this:

God is still willing to guide, to correct, and to restore. Wisdom is still available. Change is still possible. And your life still has purpose.

Walk forward with intention.

Guard what God is rebuilding.

And finish strong.

— Elder Joel Latimore Jr.

ABOUT THE AUTHOR

Elder Joel Latimore Jr. is an ordained pastor, Bible teacher, and author committed to proclaiming the faithfulness of God in the face of impossible circumstances.

His writing is grounded in Scripture, shaped by conviction, and offered with pastoral care for those navigating hardship, uncertainty, and spiritual struggle.

Rather than presenting theoretical faith or emotional reassurance, Elder Latimore writes to point readers toward **repentance, obedience,** and **dependence** on the Holy Ghost—the sustaining presence of God given to believers.

His work consistently emphasizes **spiritual maturity, accountability,** and **the reality that God remains active in the lives of those who trust Him.**

His ministry and writing reflect a lifelong commitment to biblical clarity and honest faith, particularly for those who feel overlooked, burdened, or unsure of their future. He believes Scripture speaks plainly, that God is faithful, and that no circumstance—past or present—is beyond the reach of God's power and grace.

Elder Latimore is the author of multiple faith-based works focused on discipleship, endurance, repentance, and spiritual growth. Through his writing, he encourages readers to trust God fully, walk by faith, and believe—without reservation—that there is nothing too hard for the Lord.

www.ingramcontent.com/pod-product-compliance
Lightning Source LLC
Chambersburg PA
CBHW051954150726
47999CB00004B/1384